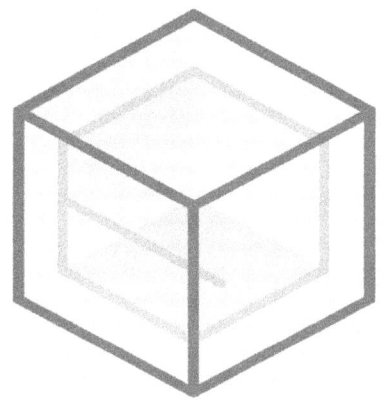

Scaffolding Agency

Structure, Persistence, and Agency

Third Edition

Drexler Rugs

DISCLAIMER

This book is an explanatory and analytical work concerned with how learning, structure, and agency are experienced and understood. It does not provide instruction, training, techniques, or methods of any kind, nor does it prescribe actions, interventions, or practices.

Nothing in this book is intended to diagnose, treat, modify, or intervene in any medical, psychological, psychiatric, or therapeutic condition. The discussion of cognition, learning, and agency is conceptual and phenomenological, not clinical or procedural.

This book does not establish a professional, instructional, or advisory relationship between the author and the reader.

Scope and Boundaries

The work presented in my books and public writing is **descriptive and analytical**, not prescriptive. Accordingly:

- I do **not** provide psychological, psychiatric, or therapeutic services.
- I do **not** offer coaching, counseling, or guided cognitive interventions.
- I do **not** facilitate identity reconstruction, belief modification, or emotional processing.
- I do **not** claim authority over individual learning outcomes or personal transformation.
- I do **not** provide individualized guidance for cognitive or behavioral change.
- I do **not** advocate or endorse undisclosed, non-consensual, or covert cognitive influence.
- I do **not** recommend the application of cognitive scaffolding without informed understanding, agency, and the ability to disengage.
- I do **not** position my work as a substitute for education, therapy, or professional training.
- I do **not** license others to apply my concepts as techniques, methods, or interventions in applied settings.
- I do **not** claim empirical validation for subjective or phenomenological outcomes described in my work.

Responsibility and Use

- Readers are responsible for how they interpret and apply ideas discussed in my writing.
- Any practical use of these concepts should be undertaken with explicit consent, transparency, and appropriate professional oversight.

My role is limited to **clarifying structures, conditions, and risks**, not directing action.

Copyright © 2026 Drexler Rugs

All rights reserved.

No part of this publication may be reproduced, stored, or transmitted in any form or by any means, electronic or mechanical, without prior written permission of the author, except for brief quotations used in reviews or scholarly commentary.

ISBN: 979-8-9930752-3-5

Library of Congress Control Number: 2026902030

Volume 3 of the Cognitive Literacy series

Third Edition

Contents

Scope of Inquiry vii

SECTION I

Introduction to Scaffolding Agency 3

Chapter 1 – Agency as Experience, Not Capacity 5

Chapter 2 – The Cultural Demand for Agency 9

Chapter 3 – When Agency Is Taken for Granted 13

Glossary 17

SECTION II

Chapter 4 – Persistence as the Precondition 21

Chapter 5 – Scaffolding as Structural Condition 25

Chapter 6 – Influence Without Direction 29

Chapter 7 – From Structure to Sense 33

Note on Recognition 37

SECTION III

Chapter 8 – Agency as a Lived Effect 41

Chapter 9 – Responsibility After Explanation 45

Chapter 10 – Authority, Expertise, and Control 49

Chapter 11 – When Scaffolds Shift 53

Chapter 12 – Why Scaffolding Is Difficult to See 57

Re-Orienting Note – Recognition and Discomfort 61

CONCLUSION

Conclusion – Recognition Without Prescription 67

Appendix A – Conceptual Map 69

Scope of Inquiry

This book is concerned with how agency comes to be experienced, not with how it should be exercised.

The scope of inquiry here is explanatory rather than practical. It examines the conditions under which learning environments shape cognition, how structure stabilizes over time, and how agency is experienced once those structures are in place. The focus is not on improvement, optimization, or intervention, but on understanding.

This distinction matters. Many discussions of learning and agency move quickly toward application. They ask what should be taught, how systems should be designed, or how individuals should adapt. This book pauses before those questions. Its scope is to clarify what is already happening before any response is considered.

Level of Explanation

The level of explanation in this work is structural and phenomenological.

Structural, in that it examines how persistent environments organize cognition prior to awareness or choice. Phenomenological, in that it takes seriously how agency is lived and felt once those structures have stabilized. These two levels are held together throughout the book, not as competing perspectives, but as complementary ones.

What this book does not do is move into procedural explanation. It does not describe steps, techniques, or methods. It does not translate structure into instruction. Its concern is with conditions, not actions.

Readers accustomed to instructional or outcome-oriented texts may initially find this approach unfamiliar. That unfamiliarity is part of the scope. Understanding precedes response.

Agency as Experience

The term *agency* is used here in a specific sense.

Agency refers to the lived experience of authorship, intention, and responsibility. It is treated as something that is felt rather than something that is possessed. This book does not argue for or against philosophical positions on free will, nor does it attempt to resolve debates about determinism or autonomy.

Those debates operate at a different level.

Here, agency is approached as an experiential phenomenon that emerges once cognitive scaffolding is in place. The question is not whether agency is "real," but how it comes to feel real, stable, and personal.

This focus allows the book to examine agency without either dismissing it as illusion or elevating it as a metaphysical absolute.

Learning as Environment

Learning is treated throughout this work as environmental rather than episodic.

Rather than occurring in discrete moments of instruction, learning unfolds through sustained exposure to structured conditions. Attention, perception, and meaning are shaped not by isolated events, but by what persists. Over time, these conditions reorganize cognition, often without being noticed as learning at all.

This environmental view of learning reframes familiar experiences. What is often attributed to effort, motivation, or aptitude can be understood instead as the outcome of persistence and structure. This shift in perspective is central to the book's inquiry.

Importantly, this reframing does not deny individual experience. It explains its formation.

Reader Orientation

This book is written for readers willing to engage explanation without immediately seeking application.

It does not require agreement, but it does require patience. Many of the claims made here are not provocative in themselves; what may feel unfamiliar is the refusal to move quickly toward solutions or recommendations.

Readers may find themselves recognizing aspects of their own experience without being told what to do about them. That recognition is intentional. The book does not ask readers to adopt a position or follow a path. It asks only that they notice what has already been shaping their experience.

Why Scope Matters

Clarifying scope is not an exercise in limitation. It is an act of orientation.

By understanding the level at which this book operates, readers can engage it on its own terms. Explanation can be evaluated without expecting prescription. Recognition can occur without pressure to respond.

What follows in the chapters ahead builds on this orientation. Structure, persistence, and scaffolding are examined not to produce action, but to make visible what has long been functioning quietly in the background of learning and agency.

Transition

With the scope of inquiry established, the chapters that follow can proceed without distraction.

The work now turns fully to explanation—how structure persists, how scaffolding forms, and how agency is experienced once the ground is already built.

x

SECTION I

Agency as Experience

This section examined agency not as a possession or capacity, but as a lived certainty. By suspending assumption and tracing what disappears when agency is taken for granted, SECTION I prepared the ground for structural explanation.

Agency is not the source of learning or action, but the experience that emerges once cognitive scaffolding is established under persistence. Human cognition naturally scaffolds information over time; modern technological environments formalize and stabilize this process. As structure persists, scaffolding takes hold, and agency is experienced as personal, voluntary, and self-authored. This book explains agency not as a capacity to be cultivated, but as a phenomenological outcome of structural conditions that precede awareness and choice.

PHILOSOPHY
Noun: **phenomenology**
The science of phenomena as distinct from that of the nature of being.
 An approach that concentrates on the study of consciousness and the objects of direct experience.

Introduction to Scaffolding Agency

Why Agency Feels Personal

Agency is one of the most taken-for-granted experiences of modern life. Decisions feel owned. Intentions feel authored. Actions feel voluntary. We experience ourselves as the origin of our choices, even when we cannot fully account for how those choices came to be formed.

This book begins from a simple observation: **the experience of agency is real, but its origin is rarely examined.** Agency is typically treated as an inherent human capacity—something to be developed, protected, or exercised—rather than as an experience that emerges under specific structural conditions. When agency is assumed rather than explained, inquiry stops where it should begin.

Scaffolding Agency does not ask how people can become more agentic. It asks how agency comes to be experienced at all.

Across modern learning environments—technological, institutional, and cultural—cognitive structures are formed prior to awareness and prior to choice. These structures persist over time, organizing perception, stabilizing meaning, and shaping how information is processed. As persistence accumulates, scaffolding takes form. And once scaffolding is in place, agency is experienced.

This experience is not illusory. It is not false. But it is **structurally produced**.

The human mind already scaffolds. Long before formal systems intervene, cognition organizes information through repetition, patterning, and stabilization. What modern technologies introduce is not scaffolding itself, but **durable, externalized, and interoperable scaffolding**—structures that persist beyond individual moments and quietly guide cognition beneath awareness.

When scaffolding becomes stable enough, agency emerges as a lived certainty. Choice feels self-authored. Intention feels personal. Responsibility feels grounded. Yet the conditions that make this experience possible are rarely visible from within it.

This book examines agency as a phenomenological effect of scaffolding under persistence. It traces how structure precedes agency, how influence accumulates without instruction, and why agency is experienced as personal even when its origins are distributed, environmental, and largely unseen.

Nothing in this book aims to correct, optimize, or moralize agency. Explanation does not negate responsibility, nor does recognition remove accountability. Instead, this work offers a framework for understanding **how agency appears**, why it stabilizes, and what follows once its structural conditions are recognized.

Chapter 1 – Agency as Experience, Not Capacity

Agency is commonly treated as a possession. We speak of having agency, lacking agency, granting agency, or taking agency away. In education, work, and technology, agency is framed as something to be cultivated—an ability that can be strengthened through training, autonomy, or empowerment. These approaches assume that agency is a capacity that belongs to the individual and can be exercised at will.

This book begins from a different position.

Agency is not approached here as a capacity to be developed, nor as a moral property to be defended. It is approached as an **experience**—one that feels immediate, personal, and self-authored, yet arises under conditions that are rarely examined.

The experience of agency is unmistakable. Decisions feel owned. Intentions feel chosen. Actions feel voluntary. Even hesitation feels like a choice. From the inside, agency appears as the most obvious fact of human cognition. It is precisely this obviousness that has protected it from inquiry.

When agency is treated as a given, explanation stops. The question is no longer *how does agency appear?* but *how can it be used well?* The distinction matters. To ask how agency appears is to investigate structure. To ask how it should be used is to assume that structure has already done its work.

This book is concerned with the former.

The Mistake of Capacity Thinking

When agency is framed as a capacity, it is implicitly located within the individual. Responsibility, authorship, and intention are understood as originating internally, even when shaped by external circumstances. Learning, in turn, is treated as something that enables better use of this capacity: more knowledge leads to better choices; more autonomy leads to stronger agency.

This framing overlooks a crucial fact: **agency is experienced only after cognition has been structured.**

Before a choice can feel owned, alternatives must be perceived. Before intention can feel deliberate, meaning must be stabilized. Before action can feel voluntary, the field of action must already be organized. These conditions are not created by agency; they are what make agency possible.

Capacity thinking reverses this order. It treats agency as primary and structure as secondary, when in fact structure precedes agency and gives rise to it.

Agency as Phenomenological Certainty

Agency does not announce itself as an effect. It announces itself as origin.

This is why agency is so resistant to explanation. From within the experience, it does not feel scaffolded, conditioned, or structured. It feels immediate. It feels self-evident. It feels personal. These qualities are not illusions; they are the phenomenological signature of agency once it has stabilized.

To describe agency as an experience is not to deny its reality. It is to locate its reality correctly.

Phenomenologically, agency is encountered as certainty. One does not reason oneself into agency; one finds oneself already acting. The sense of authorship arrives fully formed. This is not because agency is innate, but because the structures that support it are no longer visible from within the experience they produce.

Structure Before Choice

Agency does not operate in a vacuum. It depends on a field of perception that has already been shaped. Language, categories, habits, expectations, and temporal rhythms organize what can be noticed, considered, and acted upon. These structures do not instruct the individual moment by moment. They persist.

Persistence is the key condition.

As structures persist over time, they stabilize cognition. As cognition stabilizes, scaffolding takes form. Scaffolding is not an intervention; it is a condition. It does not tell the learner what to do. It makes certain forms of doing feel natural, available, and self-initiated.

Once scaffolding is in place, agency is experienced.

This is why agency feels personal even when its origins are distributed. The structures that give rise to it are not encountered as external forces. They are encountered as the background of thought itself.

Why This Distinction Matters

If agency is treated as a capacity, then learning becomes a matter of empowerment and technique. If agency is understood as an experience produced by scaffolding under persistence, then learning becomes a matter of structure.

This distinction has consequences.

It changes how responsibility is understood, without removing it. It changes how influence is recognized, without moralizing it. It changes how technology is approached, not as a tool that replaces agency, but as an environment that stabilizes the conditions under which agency is experienced.

This book does not argue that agency is false, nor that it should be dismantled. It argues that **agency is explainable**.

And explanation, properly handled, does not diminish experience. It clarifies it.

Visibility of Structure Across Time

Figure 2. *Visibility of structure across time. As persistence increases, structural influence becomes less noticeable while agency remains foregrounded in experience.*

What Follows

The chapters that follow trace this explanation step by step. They do not ask how agency can be increased, optimized, or protected. They ask how agency comes to feel real in the first place.

To answer that question, we must begin where agency itself cannot see: with persistence, structure, and scaffolding.

Chapter 2 – The Cultural Demand for Agency

Agency is not only experienced; it is required.

Modern societies do not merely assume that individuals have agency—they depend on that assumption. Institutions, technologies, and systems of accountability are built on the premise that people act intentionally, choose freely, and can be held responsible for outcomes. Agency is not treated as a question; it is treated as infrastructure.

This demand is so pervasive that it often goes unnoticed. Individuals are expected to manage their learning, curate their identities, navigate complexity, and adapt continuously to changing conditions. These expectations are framed as opportunities for self-direction, yet they function as requirements. One must appear agentic in order to participate.

The cultural insistence on agency precedes any examination of how agency arises.

Agency as a Social Requirement

Agency is embedded in modern norms of responsibility. Individuals are expected to justify decisions, explain intentions, and account for outcomes. When failures occur, explanations are sought at the level of choice: why did you decide this, why did you not act differently, why did you not anticipate the consequences?

These questions presuppose agency as a given. They do not ask whether the conditions under which decisions were made were structured in advance. They do not ask how options were framed, which alternatives were visible, or what forms of action felt available. They ask only whether the individual acted well.

In this way, agency functions as a moral anchor. It stabilizes systems of reward and blame. Without agency, responsibility cannot be distributed; without responsibility, systems lose coherence. The demand for agency is therefore not incidental—it is structural.

The Compatibility Problem

As environments grow more complex, the demand for agency intensifies rather than diminishes.

Technological systems accelerate decision-making, multiply choices, and compress time. Information arrives continuously. Contexts shift rapidly. Yet individuals are still expected to act as coherent authors of their actions across these changing conditions. The expectation is not adjusted downward to match complexity; it is raised.

This produces a compatibility problem.

The more complex the environment becomes, the more structure is required to navigate it. But the more structure that is introduced, the less visible the origins of agency become. Agency must still be experienced as personal, even when the conditions that enable it are increasingly external, distributed, and persistent.

Rather than resolving this tension, modern systems rely on it.

Agency as a Stabilizing Fiction

Agency performs a stabilizing function regardless of its origins.

When individuals experience themselves as authors of their actions, systems can treat outcomes as attributable. Learning can be framed as self-directed. Adaptation can be described as personal growth. Responsibility can be assigned without interrogating structure.

This does not mean that agency is false. It means that agency is **functional**.

The experience of agency allows systems to operate smoothly. It localizes accountability, even when causality is diffuse. It preserves the appearance of autonomy, even when choice is shaped by persistent scaffolds. In this sense, agency stabilizes modern life not by explaining it, but by simplifying it.

Why Explanation Is Deferred

If agency is functionally necessary, explaining it becomes risky.

To examine the conditions that give rise to agency is to expose the scaffolding that supports responsibility, authority, and expertise. Such examination threatens to destabilize assumptions that institutions rely upon. As a result, inquiry is often redirected toward performance: how to increase agency, how to motivate learners, how to empower individuals.

These approaches preserve the demand for agency while avoiding its explanation.

What is lost in this deferral is clarity. Without understanding how agency is produced, systems mistake effects for causes. Interventions target motivation instead of structure. Failures are attributed to individuals rather than environments. The demand for agency intensifies precisely where agency is most structurally constrained.

Preparing the Ground

This book does not seek to resolve the cultural demand for agency. It seeks to explain how that demand is met.

Agency persists not because individuals are endlessly capable, but because environments are structured to produce the experience of agency under persistence. The next chapters turn away from cultural expectation and toward the conditions that make agency possible at all.

To understand agency, we must step beneath demand and examine structure.

Chapter 3 – When Agency Is Taken for Granted

Agency becomes most powerful when it is no longer noticed.

Once the experience of agency stabilizes, it recedes into the background of cognition. Decisions continue to feel owned. Intentions continue to feel personal. Actions continue to feel voluntary. But the conditions that make these experiences possible are no longer available to reflection. Agency is not examined because it appears self-evident.

This taken-for-granted quality is not accidental. It is the mark of successful scaffolding.

When structures persist long enough, they no longer appear as structures. They appear as the natural order of thought.

The Disappearance of Structure

When agency is assumed, structure disappears from explanation.

Choices are evaluated without examining how options were framed. Intentions are interpreted without considering how meaning was stabilized. Responsibility is assigned without tracing the persistence that made certain actions feel available and others unthinkable.

This disappearance does not mean structure is absent. It means structure is **functioning**.

Scaffolding that fails is visible. Scaffolding that succeeds becomes invisible.

The Shortcut of Attribution

Taking agency for granted simplifies explanation.

If individuals are assumed to be the origin of their actions, outcomes can be attributed quickly. Success and failure can be localized. Learning can be described as effort. Adaptation can be described as motivation. The complexity of environments is collapsed into the language of choice.

This shortcut is efficient. It is also misleading.

Attribution replaces inquiry. Once agency is named as the cause, investigation stops. The deeper question—*what conditions made this action feel possible?*—is no longer asked.

What Is Lost When Agency Is Assumed

When agency is treated as a given, several forms of understanding are foreclosed.

First, influence becomes difficult to recognize. If action is presumed self-authored, the accumulation of subtle, persistent influences disappears from view.

Second, responsibility becomes brittle. Without understanding how structure shapes agency, responsibility is either over-assigned to individuals or defensively rejected altogether.

Third, learning is mischaracterized. Learning appears as acquisition or effort rather than as the gradual stabilization of structure under persistence.

None of these losses are intentional. They are the cost of not examining what feels obvious.

The Comfort of Obviousness

Agency is comforting precisely because it feels immediate.

To experience oneself as an agent is to experience coherence. It provides continuity across time, justifies decisions, and supports identity. Questioning agency can feel destabilizing, not because agency is false, but because it is foundational to how experience is organized.

For this reason, agency is rarely interrogated from within experience. It is protected by familiarity. The mind does not naturally examine the conditions that make its own coherence possible.

This is why explanation must proceed indirectly.

Closing

SECTION I has not argued against agency. It has suspended assumption.

By treating agency as an experience rather than a capacity, by locating its emergence in structure and persistence, and by showing what disappears when agency is taken for granted, these chapters prepare the ground for what follows.

SECTION II turns away from experience and toward **structure itself**.

To understand how agency is experienced, we must now examine how scaffolding forms, stabilizes, and persists beneath awareness.

Glossary

SECTION I

Agency
The lived experience of authorship, intention, and voluntary action. In this work, agency is treated not as an inherent capacity or skill, but as a phenomenological effect that emerges once cognitive scaffolding is established under persistence.

Scaffolding
The structural organization of cognition that stabilizes perception, meaning, and action over time. Scaffolding is not instruction or guidance; it is a condition that shapes what feels available, natural, and self-initiated.

Persistence
The temporal continuity through which structures endure, repeat, and stabilize. Persistence is the precondition for scaffolding, allowing influence to accumulate without explicit instruction.

Structure
The patterned organization of perception, meaning, and action that precedes awareness and choice. Structure is not experienced directly once stabilized; it forms the background against which agency is felt.

Influence
The gradual shaping of cognition through repeated exposure, constraint, and reinforcement. Influence operates beneath awareness and accumulates over time through persistence.

Phenomenological
Concerned with lived experience as it is encountered from within consciousness. In this work, phenomenological analysis is used to explain how agency feels real and self-authored, without treating that experience as its own cause.

Capacity
A commonly assumed property of individuals referring to their ability to act independently or intentionally. This work distinguishes capacity from experience and does not treat agency as a capacity to be developed or trained.

SECTION II

Structure and Persistence

This section examines how cognitive scaffolding forms, stabilizes, and persists beneath awareness. Turning away from experience and toward structure itself, SECTION II traces the conditions under which agency then becomes possible.

Chapter 4 – Persistence as the Precondition

Structure does not emerge all at once. It requires time.

Before scaffolding can form, cognition must encounter continuity. Perception must repeat. Patterns must endure. Meaning must be reinforced across moments rather than discovered in isolation. This temporal condition—persistence—is the precondition for every structure examined in this book.

Without persistence, influence dissipates. With persistence, influence accumulates.

Why Time Matters More Than Choice

Agency is often explained through moments of decision. Persistence operates before those moments appear.

Choices feel meaningful only because they occur against a background that has already stabilized. Language, categories, expectations, and habits do not arise through single acts of will. They arise through repeated exposure, sustained constraint, and continuity across time.

Persistence is not duration alone. It is **repetition with coherence**.

A single experience rarely reshapes cognition. A persistent environment does.

The Accumulation of Influence

Influence does not announce itself as influence.

It arrives gradually, through exposure that feels ordinary rather than directive. Over time, what was once noticeable becomes familiar. What was once effortful becomes automatic. What was once external becomes assumed.

This accumulation does not require instruction. No explicit lesson is necessary. Persistence does the work.

The longer a structure persists, the less it is experienced as structure.

Stability Without Awareness

Persistence produces stability even when awareness is absent.

Cognitive systems adapt to what remains consistent. Attention is shaped by what recurs. Meaning is assigned based on what endures. Over time, cognition reorganizes itself around stable conditions, regardless of whether those conditions are acknowledged.

This reorganization is not experienced as learning. It is experienced as normalcy.

What persists becomes the baseline against which all else is measured.

Persistence and the Illusion of Neutrality

Because persistent structures fade from awareness, they often appear neutral.

Environments that endure are treated as natural. Constraints that remain constant are interpreted as givens. The absence of change is mistaken for the absence of influence.

This illusion is powerful.

Persistence hides causality by removing contrast. When there is nothing to compare against, structure becomes invisible.

Preparing for Scaffolding

Persistence alone does not produce scaffolding, but without persistence, scaffolding cannot form.

Scaffolding requires:

- continuity across time
- repetition without disruption
- stability sufficient to reorganize cognition

Once these conditions are met, structure begins to consolidate. Perception aligns. Meaning stabilizes. Action becomes patterned.

Only then does scaffolding emerge as a condition rather than an intervention.

Where This Leads

Understanding persistence is necessary to understand scaffolding.

The next chapter examines how persistent structures transition into scaffolds—how stability becomes organization, and how organization becomes the background against which agency is later experienced.

Persistence prepares the ground.
Scaffolding then builds upon it.

Chapter 5 – Scaffolding as Structural Condition

Scaffolding is often misunderstood as support.

In educational, organizational, and technological contexts, scaffolding is typically described as assistance provided to help learners perform tasks they could not complete on their own. In this framing, scaffolding is temporary, instrumental, and deliberately applied. Once competence is achieved, the scaffold is removed.

This book uses the term differently.

Scaffolding here does not refer to guidance, instruction, or support. It refers to a **structural condition** that emerges when persistent environments reorganize cognition. Scaffolding is not something added to learning; it is what learning becomes once structure stabilizes under persistence.

Scaffolding Is Not Instruction

Instruction presupposes an agent who receives it.

Scaffolding does not. It does not tell the learner what to do, what to value, or what to choose. It does not appear as direction. It appears as **availability**. Certain actions feel natural. Certain interpretations feel obvious. Certain paths feel self-initiated.

Nothing in this process requires explicit teaching.

This is why scaffolding often goes unrecognized. Because it does not announce itself as influence, it is mistaken for autonomy.

When Structure Becomes Scaffold

Structure becomes scaffolding when it ceases to be encountered as structure.

At earlier stages, patterns may be noticed as constraints. Repetition may feel external. Stability may feel imposed. Over time, as persistence continues, these features recede from awareness. They no longer feel like conditions; they feel like the normal background of thought.

At this point, structure has crossed a threshold.

It no longer shapes cognition from the outside. It organizes cognition from within.

This transition is not marked by awareness. There is no moment when scaffolding is "installed." It becomes visible only in retrospect, often when disrupted.

Scaffolding is the Reorganization of Perception

Once scaffolding is in place, perception reorganizes.

What stands out, what is ignored, what feels relevant, and what feels possible are no longer negotiated consciously. Attention aligns with structure. Meaning stabilizes. Action begins to flow without deliberation.

This is not efficiency. It's coherence.

Scaffolding produces a field in which action can occur smoothly. Within this field, agency is not experienced as constrained, but as enabled. Choice feels free precisely because the conditions that limit it are no longer experienced as limits.

Why Scaffolding Is Durable

Unlike instruction, scaffolding does not fade when attention shifts.

Because it is structural, it persists even when it is not reinforced explicitly. It shapes cognition across contexts. It carries forward into new situations. It does not require reminders or repetition once stabilized.

This durability is what allows agency to feel consistent across time. Without durable scaffolding, agency would fragment. Decisions would feel arbitrary. Intentions would lack continuity.

Scaffolding holds agency together.

Scaffolding Without Awareness

The most important feature of scaffolding is that it does not require recognition to function.

One need not understand scaffolding for it to shape cognition. In fact, scaffolding is most effective when it is not noticed. Awareness is not a prerequisite for its operation; it is a possible consequence of its disruption.

This is why scaffolding cannot be reduced to a technique. Techniques are applied. Scaffolding emerges.

Figure 1. Conceptual relationship between structure, persistence, scaffolding, and agency.

These elements coexist as conditions rather than temporal steps. Agency is shown as an experienced outcome of stabilized scaffolding, not as its origin.

What Scaffolding Makes Possible

Scaffolding does not produce agency directly. It produces the **conditions** under which agency can be experienced.

Once scaffolding is established:

- action feels self-authored
- intention feels deliberate
- responsibility feels grounded

These experiences are real. They are not illusions. But they are downstream.

Agency appears only after scaffolding has done its work.

Looking Ahead

Scaffolding explains how structure becomes capable of producing agency. It does not yet explain how influence accumulates without direction, nor how agency comes to feel personal rather than imposed.

Those questions require a closer examination of influence itself.

The next chapter turns to that examination.

Chapter 6 – Influence Without Direction

Influence is often mistaken for instruction.

When influence is visible, it is assumed to be intentional: someone teaches, persuades, or guides. When influence is subtle, it is dismissed as incidental. In both cases, influence is framed as an act directed toward an agent.

Scaffolding operates differently.

The most consequential influence in learning does not arrive as direction. It arrives as **continuity**. It accumulates without announcing itself, without requiring agreement, and without demanding attention. Over time, what persists reshapes cognition simply by remaining present.

Influence That Does Not Instruct

Instruction tells. Influence does not.

Instruction presupposes a moment of reception: a learner hears, reads, or observes something meant to be understood. Influence, as examined here, has no such moment. It does not require comprehension. It does not wait for consent. It does not depend on uptake.

It operates beneath those thresholds.

Persistent environments shape what is noticed, what is repeated, and what fades. Over time, cognition reorganizes around these regularities. The influence is real, but it is not experienced as influence.

This is why influence is often misattributed to choice.

Accumulation Without Awareness

Influence accumulates gradually.

Each exposure may appear insignificant. Each repetition may feel neutral. Each constraint may seem inconsequential. But persistence binds them together. Over time, accumulation produces change that no single moment can explain.

This accumulation is not experienced as pressure. It is experienced as familiarity.

What persists becomes trusted. What recurs becomes expected. What endures becomes assumed.

Why Direction Is the Wrong Frame

To look for direction is to look for intent.

Scaffolding does not require intent to function. Influence does not need to be purposeful to be effective. What matters is not whether influence is designed, but whether it persists.

This is why attempts to locate influence solely in explicit guidance fail. They miss the conditions that shape cognition long before guidance would be recognized as such.

Influence without direction is not weak influence. It is the strongest kind.

Influence and the Sense of Autonomy

One of the paradoxes of scaffolding is that the more effective influence becomes, the more autonomous action feels.

As scaffolding stabilizes, actions align with structure without friction. Decisions feel self-initiated. Intentions feel personal. There is no felt opposition to overcome, no external force to resist.

This is not because influence has ceased. It is because influence has succeeded.

Autonomy is experienced when structure no longer needs to announce itself.

Distributed Origins

When influence accumulates without direction, its origins become difficult to trace.

No single source can be identified. No moment of adoption can be recalled. The shaping appears to have "always been there." This distributed origin contributes to the experience of agency as self-authored.

If there is no identifiable source, authorship defaults inward.

This is not deception. It is a structural effect.

Preparing the Transition

Influence without direction explains how scaffolding forms without instruction. It does not yet explain how scaffolding gives rise to the felt certainty of agency.

That transition—from structure to sense—requires examining how stabilized influence becomes lived authorship.

The next chapter turns to that transition.

Chapter 7 – From Structure to Sense

Agency does not announce its arrival.

It is not introduced as a new capacity, nor does it emerge as a distinct event. Instead, agency appears as a shift in how action is felt. What once required deliberation begins to feel obvious. What once felt effortful begins to feel natural. Choice does not become easier; it becomes quieter.

This is the moment where structure becomes sense.

When Structure Is No Longer Encountered

As scaffolding stabilizes, cognition no longer encounters structure as external.

Patterns that were once noticeable fade into the background. Constraints that once felt imposed are no longer experienced as constraints. The environment no longer feels like something to navigate; it feels like the natural field within which action occurs.

At this point, structure has completed its work.

Nothing new has been added. Nothing has been taught. Yet experience has changed.

The Emergence of Ownership

Ownership is not claimed; it is felt.

When action aligns smoothly with stabilized structure, decisions are experienced as self-authored. Intentions feel personal not because they originate independently, but because there is no felt resistance between cognition and environment.

This absence of friction is critical.

Agency is experienced most strongly when action flows without obstruction. The less visible the scaffolding, the more complete the sense of authorship.

Sense Without Source

One of the defining features of agency is that it feels source-less.

People rarely experience their actions as emerging from accumulated influence. They experience them as arising from within. This is not a failure of introspection; it is the expected outcome of stabilized scaffolding.

When influence is distributed across time and environment, no single cause stands out. Without an identifiable source, experience resolves inward.

Agency fills the explanatory gap.

Why Agency Feels Immediate

Agency is experienced in the present, even though its conditions were established over time.

This temporal mismatch contributes to its certainty. Because the effects of scaffolding are already in place by the time action is felt, agency appears unmediated. There is no awareness of preparation, no recollection of construction.

The ground does not feel built. It feels given.

Coherence as Confirmation

Agency is reinforced by coherence.

When actions align with expectations, when outcomes make sense, and when identity feels stable across time, agency is confirmed rather than questioned. The experience of coherence retroactively justifies the sense of authorship.

This feedback loop strengthens agency without exposing its origins.

From Explanation to Recognition

To explain agency is not to undermine it.

Recognition does not remove experience; it reframes it. Once the structural conditions of agency are understood, agency can be experienced without being mistaken for its own cause.

This recognition does not dissolve responsibility or intention. It changes where explanation begins.

Closing

SECTION II has traced the conditions under which agency becomes possible without yet invoking agency itself.

Persistence establishes continuity.
Scaffolding organizes cognition.
Influence accumulates without direction.
Structure becomes sense.

Agency will appear next—not as a premise, but as an outcome.

Note on Recognition

The structures described in this section are not speculative. They are not theoretical abstractions awaiting implementation. They already operate wherever learning environments persist long enough to stabilize perception, meaning, and action.

What is changing is not the existence of scaffolding, but its **formalization**. As learning systems become more durable, interoperable, and continuous, scaffolding becomes more legible—both to those who design such systems and to those who experience their effects.

This book does not instruct readers on how to produce or enter such structures. Its purpose remains identification. Recognition precedes evaluation. Explanation precedes response.

After Recognition

Recognition alters orientation before it alters understanding.

Once scaffolding is recognized, experience does not immediately change. Agency continues to be felt. Responsibility continues to matter. Action continues to occur. What shifts is not behavior, but interpretation. Events that once felt purely personal begin to be understood as situated. Choices that once appeared self-generated are seen as supported.

This shift does not diminish agency. It relocates explanation.

Recognition does not require agreement, nor does it demand action. It introduces a pause between experience and attribution. In that pause, assumptions about authorship, autonomy, and control can be examined without being resolved.

This book does not ask readers to remain in that pause indefinitely. It asks only that the pause be acknowledged as possible.

The chapters that follow examine what happens once agency is already in place—when it is lived, relied upon, and assumed.

SECTION III

The Consequences of Agency

This section examines what follows once agency is experienced as personal and self-authored. Turning from structure to consequence, SECTION III explores how agency reshapes responsibility, authority, and coherence over time.

Chapter 8 – Agency as a Lived Effect

Agency is not encountered as an explanation.
It is encountered as a fact.

Once experienced, agency feels immediate and undeniable. Actions feel owned. Intentions feel deliberate. Responsibility feels grounded. These experiences do not arrive tentatively; they arrive with certainty. Agency does not ask to be believed. It is lived.

This chapter examines agency not as an origin, but as a **lived effect**—one that reshapes how individuals understand themselves and their actions once scaffolding has already done its work.

The Certainty of Authorship

Agency is experienced as authorship.

When actions align smoothly with stabilized structure, individuals experience themselves as the source of their choices. This experience does not feel inferred or constructed. It feels direct. The sense of "I decided" does not appear as a conclusion; it appears as a starting point.

This certainty is not fragile. It persists even when outcomes are ambiguous or unintended. Agency does not depend on success. It depends on coherence.

Agency and Identity

Once agency is experienced consistently, it becomes woven into identity.

Individuals do not merely act; they understand themselves as actors. Past decisions are integrated into narratives of self. Future actions are anticipated as expressions of intention. Agency provides continuity across time, allowing experience to be organized as a personal trajectory rather than a series of events.

This narrative stability is one of agency's most powerful effects.

Responsibility After Emergence

Responsibility follows agency, not the other way around.

Once actions are experienced as self-authored, responsibility feels natural rather than imposed. Accountability no longer appears as external judgment; it appears as alignment between intention and outcome.

This alignment does not require explicit justification. It is felt.

Importantly, explanation does not remove responsibility. Understanding how agency emerges does not negate the experience of ownership. It clarifies its conditions without dissolving its force.

When Agency Is Relied Upon

Modern systems rely on agency once it is in place.

Institutions assume that individuals will act intentionally, manage complexity, and adapt to change. The experience of agency allows these expectations to feel reasonable. Without agency, demands would feel coercive. With agency, they feel self-directed.

This reliance reinforces agency further, embedding it deeper into experience.

The Stability of the Effect

Agency, once stabilized, is durable.

It carries across contexts. It persists through uncertainty. It adapts to new conditions without losing its sense of authorship. This durability is not the result of effort; it is the result of scaffolding that continues to hold.

Agency endures because the structures that support it endure.

Looking Ahead

If agency is a lived effect, it has consequences beyond individual experience.

The next chapters examine how agency reshapes authority, expertise, and responsibility at larger scales—how systems come to depend on experiences they do not explain, and how coherence is maintained even as structures shift.

Chapter 9 – Responsibility After Explanation

Explanation does not dissolve responsibility.

One of the most common fears surrounding structural accounts of agency is that they weaken accountability. If agency is produced by scaffolding, if choice emerges from persistent structure, then responsibility appears threatened. Actions begin to look conditioned rather than chosen, and responsibility risks being displaced onto systems, environments, or abstractions.

This concern misunderstands what explanation does.

Responsibility Does Not Precede Agency

Responsibility follows agency.

Before actions are experienced as self-authored, responsibility cannot attach. Obligation requires authorship. Accountability requires intention. Without agency, responsibility would be incoherent.

Explanation does not remove these conditions; it clarifies how they come to exist.

Once agency is experienced, responsibility is not optional. It is embedded in the same coherence that makes action feel owned. Explanation may shift where responsibility is *understood* to originate, but it does not remove the experience that grounds it.

Explanation as Expansion, Not Evasion

To explain the conditions of agency is not to excuse action.

Structural explanation expands the frame of understanding without negating the experience of choice. Individuals still act. Decisions are still made. Consequences still follow. What changes is not responsibility itself, but the depth at which responsibility can be examined.

Explanation allows responsibility to be contextualized rather than absolutized.

This contextualization is not moral leniency. It is ethical precision.

Distributed Conditions, Singular Action

While the conditions that give rise to agency may be distributed across time and environment, action is experienced singularly.

An individual acts in a moment. The experience of authorship is localized, even when its origins are not. Responsibility attaches to this localized experience, not to the abstract conditions that made it possible.

This asymmetry is unavoidable.

Explanation reveals that agency depends on structure, but responsibility attaches where agency is felt.

The Stability of Accountability

Responsibility remains stable precisely because agency is stable.

Once scaffolding has produced a durable sense of authorship, accountability does not fluctuate with awareness of structure. Knowing that agency has conditions does not cause responsibility to evaporate. It simply prevents responsibility from being misapplied.

This distinction matters.

Without explanation, responsibility is often over-assigned, placed on individuals for outcomes shaped by persistent structures beyond their control. With explanation, responsibility can be distributed more accurately—without being denied.

Responsibility Without Illusion

Structural explanation removes illusion, not obligation.

It does not claim that individuals are puppets. It does not claim that actions are meaningless. It claims that agency is explainable, and that explanation does not require disbelief.

Responsibility after explanation is not lighter; it is sharper.

It recognizes the limits of individual control without denying individual action. It allows accountability to be held without pretending that context does not matter.

Looking Ahead

If responsibility persists after explanation, other social structures do as well.

Authority, expertise, and legitimacy all depend on experienced agency. They are built on assumptions of authorship, intention, and accountability. To explain agency is to place these structures under examination—not to dismantle them, but to understand their foundations.

The next chapter turns to that examination.

Chapter 10 – Authority, Expertise, and Control

Authority depends on agency.

Institutions function on the assumption that individuals can act intentionally, understand directives, and take responsibility for outcomes. Expertise is recognized where judgment is trusted. Control is exercised where compliance appears voluntary. None of these structures operate without the experience of agency as their foundation.

This chapter examines how authority, expertise, and control rely on agency once it is already in place—and how structural explanations of agency complicate, but do not invalidate, these arrangements.

Authority as Delegated Agency

Authority is rarely experienced as force. It is experienced as delegation.

When individuals accept authority, they do so not because they lack agency, but because their agency aligns with the structures that authorize direction. Instructions feel legitimate when they fit within an already scaffolded field of understanding.

Authority succeeds when it does not need to assert itself.

This is why authority often appears natural rather than imposed. It operates through alignment, not coercion.

Expertise and the Organization of Judgment

Expertise depends on the stabilization of judgment.

To recognize expertise is to trust that someone can see, interpret, and decide in ways that others cannot. This trust presupposes agency: the expert is assumed to act intentionally, responsibly, and with understanding.

Yet expertise itself is scaffolded.

What counts as relevant information, valid interpretation, or appropriate action is shaped by persistent structures within a domain. Expertise emerges where scaffolding has stabilized perception and meaning sufficiently to support reliable judgment.

Expertise feels personal, but it is structurally supported.

Control Without Force

Control is most effective when it is least visible.

Systems that rely on overt coercion are fragile. Systems that align agency with structural expectations are stable. When individuals experience their actions as self-directed, control does not need to be enforced; it is enacted.

This does not require deception. It requires scaffolding.

Once the conditions that produce agency are in place, behavior aligns with structure without resistance. Control is experienced as choice.

The Asymmetry of Explanation

Explaining the structural conditions of agency introduces asymmetry.

Those who understand how agency is scaffolded gain insight into how authority and expertise are maintained. Those who experience agency without examining its origins remain subject to its effects without recognizing their source.

This asymmetry does not automatically imply manipulation or abuse. It does, however, create differential visibility.

Authority operates most smoothly where its structural foundations remain unseen.

Authority After Explanation

Structural explanation does not abolish authority.

Institutions do not cease to function once agency is explained. Expertise does not dissolve. Control does not vanish. What changes is the possibility of reflection.

Explanation introduces the option to distinguish between legitimacy and inevitability, alignment and consent, coherence and compliance.

This distinction does not prescribe action. It clarifies structure.

Looking Ahead

If authority and expertise depend on experienced agency, they are sensitive to changes in scaffolding.

When structures shift, legitimacy shifts with them. When scaffolding destabilizes, authority becomes visible—and contested. Understanding these dynamics is essential for navigating environments where learning, decision-making, and responsibility are increasingly structured rather than instructed.

The final chapter examines what happens when scaffolding no longer holds—when drift, rupture, and instability expose the conditions that once remained invisible.

Chapter 11 – When Scaffolds Shift

Scaffolding is most visible when it fails.

As long as structures remain stable, agency feels continuous and self-authored. Authority feels legitimate. Expertise feels reliable. Control feels aligned with choice. These experiences depend on scaffolding holding quietly in the background.

When scaffolding shifts, this quiet coherence is disrupted.

Drift, Rupture, and Misalignment

Scaffolds do not always collapse suddenly.

More often, they drift. Structures that once aligned perception and action begin to misfit changing conditions. Familiar cues lose relevance. Established meanings no longer stabilize experience. Actions that once felt obvious begin to feel strained.

This drift is rarely recognized immediately. Agency persists even as coherence weakens. Individuals continue to experience themselves as authors of their actions, even when outcomes feel increasingly unpredictable.

The Exposure of Structure

When scaffolding destabilizes, structure becomes visible.

Constraints that were once unnoticed begin to press. Expectations that once felt natural begin to feel imposed. Authority that once aligned with agency begins to feel external. What was previously assumed now demands explanation.

This exposure can feel disorienting, not because agency disappears, but because its supporting conditions are no longer seamless.

Agency remains. The ground shifts.

The Temptation of Reassertion

When scaffolding falters, systems often respond by intensifying demands for agency.

Individuals are encouraged to adapt faster, choose better, and take greater responsibility. The assumption is that stronger agency will compensate for weakened structure. This response misunderstands the relationship between agency and scaffolding.

Agency cannot repair structure. It depends on it.

Reasserting agency where scaffolding has shifted increases friction rather than restoring coherence.

Instability as a Moment of Recognition

Moments of scaffold shift create rare opportunities for recognition.

When structure becomes visible, explanation becomes possible. The conditions that were previously invisible can be examined—not to restore the past, but to understand the present.

This recognition is not inherently destabilizing. It can clarify why agency feels strained, why authority is contested, and why coherence falters. Explanation does not solve these conditions, but it changes how they are encountered.

The Persistence of Agency

Even as scaffolding shifts, agency does not vanish.

Individuals continue to experience themselves as actors. Responsibility continues to be felt. Choice continues to occur. What changes is the reliability of alignment between agency and outcome.

This persistence is important. It prevents collapse. But it also masks the need for structural understanding.

Agency survives disruption, but it cannot correct it.

Closing

SECTION III has examined what follows once agency is established as a lived effect.

Responsibility persists after explanation.
Authority and expertise rely on experienced agency.
Control operates through alignment rather than force.
And when scaffolding shifts, the conditions that support agency are exposed.

What remains is not a solution, but an orientation.

Chapter 12 – Why Scaffolding Is Difficult to See

Scaffolding is difficult to see because it works.

Structures that succeed in organizing cognition do so by removing themselves from attention. Once stabilized, they no longer appear as conditions. They appear as the natural background of thought, perception, and action.

What is most effective is rarely most visible.

The Disappearance of Structure

When structure is new, it can feel constraining.

Patterns are noticeable. Repetition is felt. Alignment requires effort. At this stage, structure may be experienced as external or imposed. Over time, as persistence continues, this experience changes. Structure recedes from awareness. What was once noticed becomes assumed.

This disappearance is not failure. It is completion.

A scaffold that remains visible has not yet done its work.

Familiarity as Concealment

Familiarity conceals causality.

As environments persist, cognition adapts to them. Attention aligns. Meaning stabilizes. What recurs becomes expected, and what is expected no longer stands out. The conditions shaping experience are no longer interrogated because they no longer appear variable.

This concealment is not cognitive error. It is a functional adaptation.

To notice structure requires contrast. Persistence removes contrast.

Why Agency Masks Scaffolding

Agency further obscures scaffolding.

Once action feels self-authored, attention shifts away from conditions and toward intention. Decisions are experienced as originating within the self rather than emerging from stabilized structure. This inward resolution feels accurate because it is experientially coherent.

Scaffolding does not compete with agency. It supports it.

As a result, the more complete the scaffolding, the more convincing the experience of autonomy.

The Problem of Retrospective Explanation

Scaffolding is difficult to reconstruct after the fact.

Because it forms gradually and without instruction, there is rarely a moment to point to. No single influence can be isolated. No origin can be identified. Retrospective explanation encounters a smooth surface where process once occurred.

This smoothness leads to misattribution.

What feels continuous is assumed to be innate. What feels personal is assumed to be self-generated. The absence of memory becomes evidence of absence.

Discomfort as a Signal

When scaffolding is named, discomfort often follows.

This discomfort does not arise because the explanation is wrong, but because it disrupts assumed authorship. To suggest that agency has conditions is to unsettle a deeply held orientation, not merely a belief.

Resistance is therefore predictable.

It is easier to accept constraint than to accept condition. Constraint can be opposed. Condition must be recognized.

Recognition Without Collapse

Seeing scaffolding does not dismantle it.

Recognition does not undo structure, nor does it remove agency. It reframes understanding. What changes is not how one acts, but how one explains action.

This distinction matters.

Scaffolding is difficult to see because it is not designed to be seen. It is designed to hold.

Looking Ahead

If scaffolding is difficult to see, then recognizing it requires a particular posture—one that resists instruction, avoids prescription, and tolerates ambiguity.

```
Experience
AGENCY
Explanation
Structure · Persistence · Scaffolding
```

Explanation and lived experience operate at different levels.
Recognition reframes interpretation without dismantling agency as it is experienced

The final sections of this book turn toward that posture, examining what recognition makes possible without turning explanation into action.

Re-Orienting Note – Recognition and Discomfort

Recognition is rarely comfortable.

To recognize scaffolding is not to learn something new, but to notice something that has been operating quietly for a long time. This kind of recognition does not arrive as insight alone. It often arrives accompanied by tension, resistance, or unease.

That discomfort is not incidental. It is structural.

When Explanation Interrupts Coherence

Much of everyday experience depends on coherence. Actions feel aligned. Intentions feel clear. Responsibility feels grounded. These experiences are supported by scaffolding that remains invisible as long as it holds.

Recognition interrupts this invisibility.

When scaffolding is named, the seamless background of experience is briefly disturbed. What once felt given now appears conditioned. What once felt entirely self-authored now appears supported. This interruption can feel destabilizing, even when no action is required.

Discomfort is the signal that coherence has been touched, not that it has been destroyed.

Why Recognition Feels Personal

Recognition often feels personal because it reaches beneath beliefs and preferences.

Scaffolding shapes how meaning is assigned, how relevance is perceived, and how action feels possible. When these conditions are made visible, the interruption is not merely intellectual. It is experiential.

Readers may feel that something about their own agency has been questioned. This is not because agency has been denied, but because its conditions have been illuminated.

Experience resists explanation when explanation arrives too close to its foundations.

The Temptation to Resolve

Discomfort invites resolution.

When faced with unsettling explanation, it is common to seek:

- reassurance,
- instruction,
- or an alternative framework that restores certainty.

This book deliberately resists offering such resolution.

Recognition does not require repair. It requires tolerance. The discomfort associated with recognition often fades as explanation is integrated, not because the explanation is rejected, but because experience adapts to understanding.

Recognition Without Demand

This interlude is not an invitation to act.

It does not ask readers to change how they learn, how they decide, or how they understand themselves. It acknowledges that recognition can feel consequential even when no response is prescribed.

Not every insight requires action. Some require only orientation.

Holding the Tension

To recognize scaffolding is to hold a tension between explanation and experience.

Agency continues to be felt. Responsibility continues to matter. Meaning continues to be made. Recognition does not erase these realities. It reframes them.

The discomfort that accompanies this reframing is temporary. The orientation it provides can be durable.

Transition

What follows is not instruction, and not intervention.

The conclusion that follows closes this inquiry by reaffirming its posture: explanation without prescription, recognition without demand, and understanding without coercion.

CONCLUSION

Recognition Without Prescription

Conclusion – Recognition Without Prescription

This work offers orientation rather than instruction.

Recognition precedes response.

Instruction	Orientation
Method	Recognition
Technique	Explanation
Optimization	Understanding
Training	Awareness

This book has not argued against agency.
It has explained it.

By tracing how persistence stabilizes structure, how scaffolding organizes cognition, and how agency is experienced once these conditions are in place, this work has reframed what is often taken as self-evident. Agency has been treated not as an origin, but as an outcome—real, lived, and consequential, yet structurally produced.

Nothing in this explanation requires disbelief.

Agency remains experienced as personal. Responsibility remains felt. Authority, expertise, and control continue to operate. Explanation does not negate these realities; it clarifies their conditions. What changes is not experience itself, but where understanding begins.

This book has intentionally avoided instruction. It does not offer methods for shaping cognition, improving agency, or navigating structural change. Prescription would collapse explanation into action, and action is not the task here.

Recognition is.

To recognize scaffolding is not to escape it. To understand agency is not to transcend it. Recognition does not confer control. It confers orientation.

That orientation matters because learning environments are becoming more persistent, more structured, and more continuous. As scaffolding becomes increasingly formalized, the experience of agency will remain central to how individuals understand themselves and their actions—even as the conditions that produce that experience become less visible.

This work does not resolve that tension. It names it.

What follows from recognition is not dictated. Response belongs to contexts, institutions, and individuals beyond the scope of explanation. The contribution of this book is to ensure that such responses are not made in ignorance of the structures that already shape them.

Agency will continue to be experienced.
Structure will continue to persist.
Scaffolding will continue to organize cognition.

This book ends where those realities meet—without prescription, and without illusion.

What Recognition Changes

Recognition changes where explanation begins.

Without recognition, agency is taken as an origin. With recognition, agency is understood as an experience supported by conditions that persist beyond awareness. This shift does not resolve questions of responsibility or intention. It reframes them.

What changes is not the demand placed on individuals, but the stories used to explain why action feels possible, necessary, or inevitable. Recognition allows those stories to be examined without requiring them to be replaced.

This examination does not prescribe response. It creates space for discernment.

The purpose of this book has been to open that space.

Appendix A – Conceptual Map

This appendix provides a conceptual orientation to the key relationships explored in this book. It does not introduce new arguments or claims. Its purpose is to clarify how central concepts relate to one another once the main inquiry has been completed.

Structure and Persistence

Structure refers to the patterned organization of perception, meaning, and action. Persistence is the condition that allows structure to stabilize over time. Without persistence, patterns dissolve. With persistence, patterns endure long enough to reorganize cognition.

Structure is not imposed in moments. It is established through continuity.

Scaffolding and Influence

Scaffolding emerges when persistent structure organizes cognition from within rather than appearing as an external constraint. Influence accumulates through repetition and stability, not through instruction or direction.

Once scaffolding is in place, influence no longer feels external. It becomes the background against which agency is experienced.

Agency and Experience

Agency is treated in this work as a lived experience rather than a capacity or possession. It is experienced as authorship, intention, and responsibility. Agency does not precede scaffolding; it emerges once scaffolding has stabilized.

This experiential reality remains intact even when its conditions are explained.

Recognition and Explanation

Recognition refers to the act of noticing the structural conditions that support experience. Explanation provides a framework for understanding those conditions without prescribing action.

Recognition does not dismantle experience. It reorients interpretation.

Orientation Without Prescription

Throughout this work, explanation is offered without instruction. The conceptual relationships described here are not presented as techniques or methods. They are offered as orientation—ways of understanding what is already occurring within learning environments and lived experience.

The absence of prescription is intentional.

www.ingramcontent.com/pod-product-compliance
Lightning Source LLC
Chambersburg PA
CBHW051325110526
44582CB00004B/101